D0941219

A BLUE BANNER BIOGRAPHY

Ritchie Valens

By John Bankston

Mitchell Lane
PUBLISHERS

P.O. Box 196
Hockessin, Delaware 19707
Visit us on the web: www.mitchelllane.com
Comments? email us: mitchelllane@mitchelllane.com

Blue Banner Biographies

Eminem	Sally Field	Jodie Foster
Melissa Gilbert	Rudy Giuliani	Ron Howard
Michael Jackson	Nelly	Mary-Kate and Ashley Olsen
Daniel Radcliffe	Shirley Temple	**Ritchie Valens**
Rita Williams-Garcia		

Library of Congress Cataloging-in-Publication Data
Bankston, John, 1974-
        Ritchie Valens / John Bankston.
             p. cm. – (Blue banner biography)
Summary: A brief biography of the young singer from California who became the first Latino rock
    star, only to die in 1959, shortly after he had achieved stardom.
Includes bibliographical references (p.   ) and index.
Discography: p.
        ISBN 1-58415-186-2 (library bound)
    1. Valens, Ritchie, 1941-1959 — Juvenile literature. 2. Singers — United States — Biography —
Juvenile literature. [1. Valens, Ritchie, 1941-1959. 2. Singers. 3. Hispanic Americans — Biography.
4. Rock music.] I. Title. II. Series.
        ML3930.V25 B3 2003
        782.42166'092--dc21
                                                                                        2002014359

ABOUT THE AUTHOR: Born in Boston, Massachussetts, **John Bankston** began publishing articles in newspapers and magazines while still a teenager. Since then, he has written over two hundred articles, and contributed chapters to books such as *Crimes of Passion*, and *Death Row 2000*, which have been sold in bookstores across the world. He has written numerous biographies for young adults, including Mandy Moore and Alexander Fleming and the Story of Penicillin (Mitchell Lane). He currently lives in Portland, Oregon.
DEDICATION: To my father — a great fan of Ritchie Valens, Buddy Holly, and the Big Bopper.
PHOTO CREDITS: Cover: Shooting Star Archives/Shooting Star; p. 4 Shooting Star Archives/ Shooting Star; p. 7 Hulton/Archive; p. 20 Rochelle Law/Shooting Star International; p. 25 Rochelle Law/Shooting Star International; p. 26 Hulton/Archive; p. 27 Hulton/Archive; p. 29 AP Photo/ Kathy Willens

ACKNOWLEDGMENTS: The following story has been thoroughly researched, and to the best of our knowledge, represents a true story. While every possible effort has been made to ensure accuracy, the publisher will not assume liability for damages caused by inaccuracies in the data, and makes no warranty on the accuracy of the information contained herein. This story has not been authorized nor endorsed by Ritchie Valens.

CONTENTS

Born Ritchie Valenzuela, Ritchie Valens grew up poor but became a pop star before he was old enough to vote.

A Troubled Home

*R*itchie was shy. As friends and family gathered in his father's cramped house, he knew they were all waiting for him to sing. He didn't want to, but he knew if he didn't his father would get upset. *Very* upset. So the six-year-old moved into the center of all those grown-ups and began to sing. He wasn't very good. But he would get better.

Richard Stephen Valenzuela was born on May 13, 1941, less than an hour after midnight. When father Steve and mother Concepcion (Connie) brought baby Ritchie home, there were already problems. The couple fought constantly at their tiny home on 1337 Coronel Street, in San Fernando, California. Part of the San Fernando Valley section of Los Angeles, the town boasted a large population of

Mexican Americans, many of whom were second or third generation. Steve had been born in California, his wife in Arizona. In the Valenzuela household, English was the primary language, and Ritchie spoke little Spanish.

> **Ritchie wanted to ride a horse like his father. Since he was too small to ride a horse, he rode a sheep instead.**

What he mainly learned was how to hide, making himself as small as possible while his parents raged. His half brother, Robert Morales, was four years older and a protector to Ritchie. Robert was Connie's son, the product of a previous relationship; by the time Ritchie was three his mother was through with Steven as well.

Father and son Ritchie left together, moving to a patch of property Steve owned in neighboring Pacoima, a rougher part of the valley, where crime and gang activity were on the rise.

Although Steve was trained as a tree surgeon, he did whatever work he could find. Often he worked at a nearby ranch. Ritchie would watch in admiration as his father skillfully rode the horses. Ritchie wanted to be just like him. Since he wasn't big enough to ride a horse, he rode a sheep instead!

Ritchie saw Connie often, but it was his father Ritchie looked up to; it was his father he wanted to impress.

Above all things, what Steve Valenzuela loved was music. He loved the *corridos,* traditional Mexican folk ballads; he loved country and western; and he especially loved the singing cowboys Roy Rogers and Gene Autry, who rode horses and sang on

Ritchie's dad, Steve, enjoyed traditional Mexican ballads, but also loved popular American singers like Gene Autry (shown here).

movie theater screens in the 1930s and 1940s. Steve didn't have a very strong background in music, but he wanted his son to be successful. He believed music could be a big part of that. He encouraged Ritchie to play the guitar and even the trumpet.

Although Steve wasn't very talented musically, Connie's relatives were. In the Valenzuela household relatives were always welcome. Even after his parents' separation, Ritchie watched mesmerized at his mother's house as her side of the family played their instruments. Although it took the boy a while to get his own instrument, he made do. At three years old he wound rubber bands across the open top of a tin can; later he used a cigar box to make his own toy guitars. When Ritchie was nine years old, Steve gave him his first real guitar. By then Ritchie was already receiving regular music lessons from guitar players Uncle John Lozano and Cousin Richard Cota.

Ritchie made his own toy guitars with rubber bands wound around cigar boxes.

As a kid, Ritchie attended Pacoima Elementary School, but there wasn't a hint of his talent. He found schoolwork boring—what he really wanted to do was play music. And when Ritchie wasn't playing music, he was playing games, mainly with his close friend and next-door neighbor David Chaubet.

The two boys would dig tunnels beneath the fences around their homes, burrowing to each other's yards. David remembered Ritchie's father as a harsh disciplinarian, but someone who had a generous spirit as well. "He used to sit at the house and call me," David later told Beverly Mendheim in her book *Ritchie Valens: The First Latino Rocker.* "'Come over here and sit down to eat!' and I'd say, 'I don't wanna eat, Steve,' and he'd say, 'I don't wanna eat alone!'" David would sit down and eat.

But for Ritchie and his father there was always music. The two shared the type of bond some fathers and sons have over fishing holes or golf courses. When Ritchie first picked up a guitar, he wasn't very good; when he sang he didn't have perfect pitch. He just kept practicing, partly

Ritchie's father was a harsh disciplinarian, but also had a generous spirit.

because he loved his father, and partly because as he got older, he too loved music.

The father and son's shared love of music became a driving force for Ritchie after 1951. That was the year tragedy arrived, and his father, who'd lived a hard life, died suddenly from a stroke. Ritchie was devastated, but he could honor his father's memory every time he played the guitar.

In 1951, Ritchie's father died suddenly from a stroke. Ritchie was devastated.

"Little Richard of the Valley"

After his father's death, Ritchie Valenzuela spent a year moving from one relative's house to another. The loss of his father turned him into something of a wild child, and he started getting into trouble. It took the strong hand of his uncles to straighten him out. He attended several elementary schools, until after a year he returned to his old Pacoima home. By then his mother had moved in, along with her two small daughters, Connie and Irma. His older half brother, Robert, was there as well. The tiny house seemed more cramped than ever before.

Money was also tighter. Ritchie was very poor, and while in elementary school he became even more aware of this. Once he was invited to the birthday party of a classmate; without the money to buy her a present, he scoured a nearby dump and found a necklace to give her. The girl realized where he'd gotten it and gave it back to him.

Life for Ritchie improved after he enrolled at Pacoima Junior High School. By then he'd realized that no matter how much he suffered, music was something he could count on. Alone he was a shy teenager. With the guitar he transformed. His shop teacher, John Whitaker, remembered Ritchie well. The boy was hard to forget—he was always bringing in guitars to work on: refinishing, polishing, restringing. He took his time with the instruments, his "babies." But what the teacher remembers best was seeing the crowds of students gathered at the cafeteria or outside near the bleachers. When a teacher sees a bunch of kids yelling and cheering, they worry. "Oh! Oh! Another fight," Whitaker recalled in *The First Latino Rocker*. "But when Ritchie was involved it was always a group of kids listening to him [play guitar,] and the teachers allowed it because he was so good at it."

> *Ritchie realized that no matter how much he suffered, music was something he could count on.*

Ritchie wasn't just a good singer and guitar player. He was filled with imagination. He'd start off by singing a popular song, but then he'd change the lyrics, adding a phrase here, a new word there—sometimes he'd create entire verses. He also got the groups of kids—white, black, Asian, and Latino—to sing along and come up with their own verses to a song called "Mama Long." The kids would step up and sing their own verses, like: "Oh Mama Long, she's so fine, makes all the guys stand in line, Oh Mama Long!"

> Ritchie was filled with imagination. He'd start off by singing a popular song, but then he'd change the lyrics.

Out of all the songs Ritchie Valenzuela played before his junior high audience, one would follow him to fame and fortune. It was the only Spanish song he played: "La Bamba." He'd learned it from one of his uncles. When he taught the song's complicated chord changes to his friends, it quickly proved what a talent he'd become.

Ritchie never got up the courage to talk to girls, but he didn't have to. After he was finished playing, *they'd* talk to *him*. In class Ritchie was an average student, someone who blended in. He wasn't a cutup, or an honor student. He didn't fail and he didn't get all As. In fact, despite the crowds his playing attracted, few thought the boy they called Little Richard of the Valley (after Little Richard, a very popular and flamboyant singer) would ever make it big.

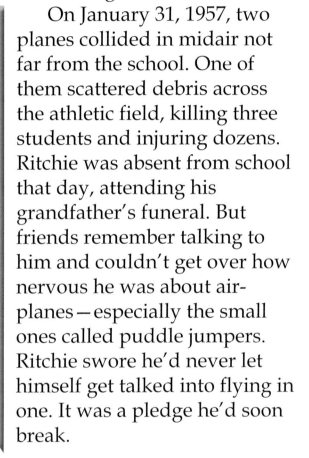

After two planes collided in midair near his school, Ritchie pledged that he'd never get talked into flying in one.

On January 31, 1957, two planes collided in midair not far from the school. One of them scattered debris across the athletic field, killing three students and injuring dozens. Ritchie was absent from school that day, attending his grandfather's funeral. But friends remember talking to him and couldn't get over how nervous he was about airplanes — especially the small ones called puddle jumpers. Ritchie swore he'd never let himself get talked into flying in one. It was a pledge he'd soon break.

The Silhouettes

*L*os Angeles in the 1950s didn't have the gang problems it does today. Still, fifty years ago L.A. had "car clubs," groups of whites or Latinos in their teens and twenties with names like the Igniters, the Drifters, and the Lobos, the largest Latino club.

"They were called car clubs, but essentially they were just gangs," admitted Louis Raring in *The First Latino Rocker.* The all-white or all-Latino clubs often got into fights over anything from cars to girls. It took a pudgy teenager who wore old jeans and a ducktail haircut to bring them a bit of peace. Ritchie Valenzuela did it the way he did most everything: with music.

Back then, Raring was a member of the Lost Angels, a white car club known for its huge parties.

The club always hired entertainment. Raring had heard Ritchie play and suggested him to the members. They weren't sure about hiring a Latino to sing at one of their parties. Then they heard Ritchie perform.

In only a few years Ritchie had developed from an awkward kid playing in cafeterias to a young man with professional skills. Although he was nervous offstage, once he got in front of an audience, he was totally comfortable. He'd start off covering the songs made famous by Little Richard, Chuck Berry, and other pop performers, but then he'd change the lyrics and the notes, making every song his own creation.

> *In only a few years Ritchie had developed from an awkward kid playing in cafeterias to a young man with professional skills.*

Ritchie was soon playing regularly for car clubs. His ability got him noticed by the Silhouettes, a cover band with a large floating roster of members in their late teens and early twenties. They invited him to play with them, although at sixteen Ritchie was one of the youngest members.

They played in and around the San Fernando Valley, mainly renting out space at local American

Legion Halls. They charged the kids who came a couple of dollars. Since there were so many members in the band, Ritchie was lucky to get ten or twenty bucks a gig.

Ritchie really needed the money. Connie was in trouble. By January 1958, her meager wages as a waitress and the one hundred fifty dollars a month she received from a pension as Steve's widow wasn't enough. (Steve and Connie's separation was never finalized by divorce.) The year before, the Valenzuela family was forced to abandon the house Steve had owned, unable to make the mortgage payments. Now Connie owed sixty-five dollars on the house she was living in—if she didn't come up with the money, her family might lose another place to live.

Playing for car clubs, Ritchie was lucky to get ten or twenty dollars a show.

Ritchie didn't want to see his family wind up on the streets or relying on handouts from relatives. He had an idea. Ritchie managed to scrape together fifty-seven dollars and rented out the Pacoima Legion Hall. He convinced his band mates to help him out, and on a Friday night kids paid two bucks apiece to see Ritchie Valenzuela play with the Silhouettes.

After expenses, Ritchie had $125. His mother would be able to pay the mortgage. But his gig did more than help out his mother. In the audience, listening to the young Little Richard of the Valley, was a talent scout for Bob Keane. In just a few short months, Bob Keane would change Ritchie's life forever.

While Ritchie performed, a talent scout for Bob Keane listened in the audience.

Fame!

*I*t took a twenty-two-year-old printer to discover the teenager they'd later call the first Latino rocker. Doug Macchia had graduated from San Fernando High—the same school Ritchie Valenzuela now attended. Macchia often went to the offices of Bob Keane, a record producer, on printing jobs.

Bob Keane came up in the world of 1940s jazz, working as a musician and later as a producer for several record labels. By the late 1950s he was ready to start his own. Keane's brainchild, Del-Fi Records, was actively seeking talent, and Ritchie Valenzuela was about to become its first star.

One day Macchia was delivering business cards for Keane, who told him to start taking a tape recorder to the rock shows he attended. Macchia be-

Although Ritchie Valens began his professional singing career as part of a band, his natural talent made him stand out. He quickly became a solo act.

gan recording the various acts he saw and playing the results for Keane. He realized finding the right act could be his break into the music business.

That break arrived when Macchia played a tape for Keane of the Silhouettes. It was from the night before, when they'd played backup as Ritchie tried to cover his mother's mortgage payment. Of all the singers Keane heard, it was Ritchie Valenzuela whose voice showed real star potential.

Of course Keane needed to see for himself. The next Saturday, he traveled with Macchia to a local movie theater where Ritchie was performing. "I'll never forget the first time I saw Ritchie," Keane later recalled. "He had a small, somewhat beat-up guitar amp worth about fifty bucks. He stood up there on stage, with complete command of his audience. He was this bull-like kid… I knew he had a lot of potential."

Bob Keane had seen a lot of singers with potential. The question was, would Ritchie Valenzuela go on to be a star?

In the 1950s, there were very few Latino artists in pop music. Signing Ritchie to a record deal was a big risk.

Unlike today, popular music like the rock and roll of the 1950s was dominated by white artists. While African-American singers like Chuck Berry and Little Richard were successful, it was the white artists who covered their songs, like Pat Boone, who sold the most albums. There were very few Latino artists in pop music, and none of them had the Spanish influence in their music that Ritchie had. Signing Ritchie to a record deal was a big risk for Keane—although he did hedge his bets. Worried that a Latino surname could hurt record sales,

Keane convinced Ritchie to take the stage name Ritchie Valens.

Keane was willing to take a chance on Ritchie, but Ritchie wasn't so sure. It wasn't that he didn't trust Keane. Ritchie was just nervous. His first recording session was scheduled for May, and when the date arrived Macchia practically had to drag Ritchie there. Macchia drove Ritchie in one car; the rest of the Silhouettes followed in another. To the boys from Pacoima, Bob Keane's house in Hollywood Hills was like another world. Any questions about how separate that world was were answered when Ritchie's band mates were stopped by the police, who didn't believe a car full of Latinos in an all-white neighborhood could be up to any good.

Ritchie was extremely nervous about his first recording session.

While Macchia dealt with the police, Ritchie went into Keane's house. He was quickly overwhelmed. The owner of Del-Fi Records had professional recording equipment in his home, along with session musicians waiting to back Ritchie up. It all made him very uncomfortable.

Ritchie stumbled through his first takes, until he convinced Keane to send the musicians out of the room. "He was not too good at first," Macchia remembered. "But he finally calmed down and the kid was just incredible. I mean, he just really got into the music and forgot everybody was there."

In that first recording session, Ritchie laid down the tracks for what would be his most famous song—"La Bamba." He also recorded another future hit, "Donna," a song about Donna Ludwig, a girl who'd broken his heart.

Over the summer of 1958, Ritchie Valens worked hard to perfect his music while Keane busily promoted the singer. Although Ritchie occasionally played with his old band mates, most of his time was devoted to his solo career.

The first Ritchie Valens single on Del-Fi records was "Come On, Let's Go." It was released in September 1958, reaching number 42 on the Billboard music charts. It would go on to sell 750,000 copies. Ritchie was on his way.

> *Ritchie stumbled through his first takes, until he convinced Keane to send the musicians out of the room.*

Winter Dance Party

*R*itchie Valens was about to become Pacoima's most famous citizen. In October 1958, Del-Fi Records released another single.

In the 1950s, singles were released on 45s, small records which spun at 45 rpms. They featured two songs, one on each side. The song the record company thought would be the hit was on the A side, the lesser song was on the B or "flip" side.

The A side of Ritchie Valens's second single was "Donna" — it would reach number two on the Billboard pop chart and make Ritchie a star. But the flip side was "La Bamba," the song Ritchie is still known for nearly fifty years later.

Around the time "Donna" was released, Ritchie dropped out of San Fernando High School to tour full-time. He would not be back.

Instead, Ritchie traveled to nearly a dozen cities on the East Coast, singing "Come On, Let's Go" and later "Donna." While today's artists rely mainly on stations like MTV for television promotion, in the fifties there were dozens of TV shows devoted to music. None was as popular for teenagers as *American Bandstand*. Filmed in Philadelphia and hosted by the youthful Dick Clark, the program would help Prince and Madonna become famous in the 1980s. When Ritchie Valens made his October 6, 1958, appearance on the program, Clark already knew about the singer's talent for improvisation. He asked the singer to make up a song with his name in it. Ritchie did it on the spot.

Donna Ludwig broke Ritchie's heart and later became immortalized in his hit song, "Donna."

For the rest of the year, Ritchie continued to tour, and even gave a concert at Pacoima Junior High. A recording of that concert was later released as an album. He also participated in promotions that were designed to turn him into a teen idol, including one called "Oh Boy, Pizza," where the winner got to have a pizza with the singer at his house. The winners of that contest remembered Valens, as nearly everyone did, as a guy who never acted like a star, even when he was one.

Dick Clark became the host of American Bandstand *while still in his twenties. For decades the show gave many performers their big break. It was Ritchie's introduction to a national audience.*

Go, Johnny, Go *was Ritchie's only movie. The film would preserve the teen star's talent long after he died.*

In January 1959, seventeen-year-old Ritchie appeared in his one and only movie, a rock and roll flick called *Go, Johnny, Go*. Ritchie was not paid for this job—it was considered promotional. Afterward he joined the Winter Dance Party. Headlined by Buddy Holly, a twenty-two-year-old singer whose hit "Peggy Sue" seemed to match well with Ritchie's hit "Donna," the tour traveled through the Midwest during the winter of 1959.

It was a very difficult gig. The weather was horrible, well below freezing. Worse, the heater on the tour bus only worked occasionally. Members of the tour began to get sick. According to "The Last Flight of Nine Four November," one band member even suffered frostbite from the ride. By February, Buddy Holly had had enough. He decided to charter a plane to Fargo, North Dakota, for him and his two guitarists. The others would take the bus.

One of his guitar players, Waylon Jennings, gave up his seat to J.P. "The Big Bopper" Richardson, who had a bad cold. The other guitarist, Tommy Allsup, flipped a coin for the remaining seat with Ritchie. Ritchie won.

No one knows why Ritchie disregarded his fear of small planes and took that flight.

The next day, February 3, the plane's owner, Jerry Dwyer, learned the group never arrived in Fargo. He got in a plane and flew over the plane's flight path. He didn't have to travel far. At about 9:30 A.M., he spotted Buddy Holly's distinctive yellow jacket from the air. As he got closer, he saw the wreckage of the plane, scattered across a farm belonging to Albert Juhl near Clear Lake. Everyone on board the plane was killed. Ritchie was found

> *While traveling for the Winter Dance Party, the heat in Ritchie's bus only worked occasionally. He decided to take a plane.*

twenty feet from the crash site, not far from Buddy Holly.

Ritchie Valenzuela's body was put on a train and sent to California. He was buried in the San Fernando Mission Cemetery.

"Ritchie was a phenomenon in many ways," Bob Keane remembers. "Unlike many entertainment stars, he will always be remembered for his gracious demeanor and sense of humor, mostly about himself."

A 1987 movie, *La Bamba,* introduced a new generation to the teenager many consider the first Latino rock and roll star.

Despite his short life, Ritchie's music has lived on. In 2001, he was inducted into the Rock and Roll Hall of Fame. Here, his family accepts his induction.

CHRONOLOGY

1941 Richard "Ritchie" Stephen Valenzuela is born on May 13 at Los Angeles County Osteopathic Hospital

1944 Ritchie's parents, Steve and Concepcion, separate; Ritchie moves with his father to Pacoima

1950 Ritchie's father gives him a guitar

1951 Ritchie's father dies; Ritchie stays with several relatives before settling in with mother Connie

1952 begins taking guitar lessons

1954 enters Pacoima Junior High

1955 begins performing for local car clubs

1957 enrolls in San Fernando High School and begins performing with the Silhouettes

1958 discovered by Bob Keane; begins using stage name Valens; his first single, "Come On, Let's Go," sells 750,000 copies; drops out of high school to tour full-time

1959 appears in film *Go, Johnny, Go;* dies in a plane crash near Clear Lake, Iowa, on February 3

1987 *La Bamba,* a movie about Ritchie's life, is released; the band Los Lobos covers the title song—it reaches number 1 on the singles chart

1993 a series of postage stamps called United States Blues and Rock Legends is released by the U.S. Post Office honoring Ritchie as one of those legends

2001 inducted into the Rock and Roll Hall of Fame

FOR FURTHER READING

George-Warren, Holly. *Shake, Rattle and Roll: The Founders of Rock and Roll.* New York: Houghton Mifflin Company, 2001.

Sinnott, Susan. *Extraordinary Hispanic Americans.* Chicago: Children's Press, 1991.

On the Web:

Ritchie Valens
    http://www.history-of-rock.com/ritchie_valens.htm

Ritchie Valens
    http://www.rockabillyhall.com/RitchieValens.html

Ritchie Valens Memorial Fan Club
    http://www.ritchievalens.net

Works Consulted:

"The Last Flight of Nine Four November"
    http://jpwright.home.texas.net/ninefour.htm

Mendheim, Beverly. *Ritchie Valens: The First Latino Rocker.* Tempe, Ariz.: Bilingual Press, 1987.

Rockabilly Hall of Fame Presentation: "Ritchie Valens."
    http://www.rockabillyhall.com/RitchieValens.html

DISCOGRAPHY

Singles		Albums	
1958	"Come On, Let's Go"	1959	*Ritchie Valens*
1958	"Donna"	1959	*Ritchie*
1958	"La Bamba"	1960	*Ritchie Valens in Concert*
1959	"That's My Little Suzie"		*at Pacoima Jr. High*

INDEX